DUELS AND DUELLING

Stephen Banks

SHIRE PUBLICATIONS

Published in Great Britain in 2012 by Shire Publications Ltd, Midland House, West Way, Botley, Oxford OX2 0PH, United Kingdom.

44-02 23rd Street, Suite 219, Long Island City, NY 11101, USA.

E-mail: shire@shirebooks.co.uk   www.shirebooks.co.uk

A CIP catalogue record for this book is available from the British Library.

Shire Library no. 683.   ISBN-13: 978 0 74781 143 5

Stephen Banks has asserted his right under the Copyright, Designs and Patents Act, 1988, to be identified as the author of this book.

Designed by Tony Truscott Designs, Sussex, UK and typeset in Perpetua and Gill Sans.

Printed in China through Worldprint Ltd.

12 13 14 15 16   10 9 8 7 6 5 4 3 2 1

COVER IMAGE
Colonel Henry and Monsieur Picquart duel during the Dreyfus Affair in France, by an unnamed artist in *Le Petit Journal*, 20 March 1898.

TITLE PAGE IMAGE
In this later depiction of the event, Giovanni Giacomo Casanova (1725–98) duels in Paris with La Tour d'Auvergne, who owes him money. Auguste Leroux, *Memoires de Casanova*.

CONTENTS PAGE IMAGE
An Anglo–French tournament at Saint-Inglevere near Calais, *c.* 1380.

ACKNOWLEDGEMENTS
I would like to thank the following for permission to use illustrations and photographs, which are acknowledged as follows:

©Heywoody/Dreamstime.com, page 30; ©Illustrated London News/Mary Evans, page 53 (top); Library of Congress, page 39; Mary Evans/AISA Media, pages 4, 14, and 48; Mary Evans/Mark Furness, page 19 (top); Mary Evans/Grosvenor Prints, page 32 (bottom); Mary Evans/Thomas H'fler/Interfoto, page 45; Mary Evans/Interfoto Agentur, pages 5 (top), 11 (top and bottom), and 12 (bottom); Mary Evans/Institute of Civil Engineers, pages 6 and 12 (top); Mary Evans/Rue des Archives/Tallandier, page 50 (top); Mary Evans/Sammlung Rauch/Interfoto, page 10 (top and bottom); Mary Evans/TV Yesterday/Interfoto, page 52 (bottom); ©McCool/Dreamstime.com, page 22 (top).

All other images are courtesy of The Mary Evans Picture Library.

Shire Publications is supporting the Woodland Trust, the UK's leading woodland conservation charity, by funding the dedication of trees.

CONTENTS

TRIAL BY BATTLE   4

THE RENAISSANCE AND THE ARRIVAL OF THE DUEL   14

THE SWORD TRIUMPHANT   20

PISTOLS AT DAWN: THE CLASSIC ENGLISH DUEL   27

THE EXTINCTION OF ENGLISH HONOUR   40

THE EUROPEAN TWILIGHT   46

FURTHER READING   55

INDEX   56

TRIAL BY BATTLE

T HE SPECTACLE of two men locked in combat has long captured the imagination. Homer's *Iliad*, recounting the Trojan War and composed sometime around the ninth century BC, is full of such contests. When Achilles chased Hector around the walls of Troy and slew him, he did so for personal honour (though the contest was decidedly uneven since the goddess Athena intervened on Achilles' side). Reputation has always been a strong motive in duels and individual combats but it is noticeable that Roman heroes, in contrast to their Greek counterparts, had to be seen to have displayed their valour in the interests of the state. Livy for example claimed that in the seventh century BC, the Roman Horatii triplets fought a duel with the Curiatii triplets from the city of Alba Longa in order to decide the outcome of a long war between them. Only one of the Horatii survived and he and his brothers were remembered ever after. That combat

Athena intervenes on the side of Achilles in the combat against Hector on this Attic black-figure cup (kylix). Archaeology Museum of Catalonia, Barcelona, Spain.

Roman gladiators
depicted in a
mosaic from the
Roman hall at
Bad Kreuznach,
Germany,
c. AD 250.

itself could be honourable was a premise shared by both Greeks and
Romans, although only the Romans developed this further by introducing
funerary games in the third century BC, at which gladiators would fight to
the death to honour the deceased.

Since many tribal peoples of Europe were illiterate, records of their
combats do not survive, but towards the end of the first millennium AD,
the rich oral tradition of Scandinavia began to result in the composition of
written sagas, tales of Norse heroes and kings. An unknown Anglo-Saxon
poet also set his tale of Beowulf and the monster Grendel in the Norse
kingdoms some time between the eighth and the early eleventh centuries
AD. A recurrent theme in the sagas is the staging by communities of formal,
rule-based contests, so called 'wagers of battle' to resolve blood feuds
between two warriors. The Norse kingdoms were at this time
predominantly pagan and Gwyn Jones, who has studied the 'holmgang' (the
Icelandic form of these combats), has remarked that in none of them did the
participants anticipate that the gods would intervene or that justice would
prevail over might or skill. The combat resolved the feud but it did not
establish whose cause had been the most just. In the Christianised kingdoms
further south however, it had long been believed that an omnipotent God
would not allow the righteous to be defeated by the unrighteous, so when
two parties had a legal dispute, one could test the merits of their respective
claims by staging a judicial combat, a 'trial by battle.'

A Norman knight depicted in a tapestry from the eleventh century, reproduced in *Norges Historie*.

For whatever reason trial by battle did not recommend itself to the Anglo Saxons. In France it was found in Burgundy as early as AD 501, but there is no reliable evidence of battle in England until Norman knights brought it with them in 1066. In 1096 William Rufus ordered a battle between Godefroy Baynard and Sir William Count d'Eu after Baynard had accused Sir William of treason. Sir William was defeated at Salisbury and was promptly castrated and blinded. In 1163 Baron Henry de Essex was forced to fight with Robert de Montford after de Montford accused him of cowardice during Henry II's campaign in Wales in 1157. De Montford claimed that Essex, the royal standard bearer, had dropped the standard and had fled after being ambushed by the Welsh. The men fought on an island in the Thames close to Reading Abbey. Essex was defeated and left for dead, but monks took him back to the Abbey, where he recovered and claimed sanctuary.

De Montford may have had a personal motive for his accusation, since he and Essex were involved in a property dispute at the time. In fact, few battles were actually fought over criminal or treasonous matters and only the most notorious were by royal command. Most were fought over disputed lands and in such civil cases forfeiture of property was at stake not the life of the litigants. Furthermore, the power to order them was vested not only in the king but also in the great feudal lords sitting in their manorial courts. Most applications for a writ of battle went before these lords and the disputants had to pay a fee for the privilege. Judicial combat was symbolic of the fragmented nature of power in Norman England. One of the measures that Henry II took in 1179 to try to strengthen the monarchy was to introduce, as an alternative to battle, the right of trial by jury before the royal judges. Thus he and his nominees garnered some of the fees and prestige that had hitherto gone to the manorial lords. Battle however, remained an option and by then the practice had evolved of appointing champions to act in place of the disputants, so rich men were able to hire others to be cleaved on their behalf.

In combat the champions would meet on foot or on horseback, but first each had to swear an oath before four knights that they would not use sorcery to prevail. A wise precaution, since when the champions of the Bishop of

Salisbury and the Earl of Salisbury fought in 1355, the bishop's man was found to have been equipped with black magic spells! Champions were liable to be fined if they showed cowardice on the field, but it seems that in civil cases few were killed outright, although this did happen in the case of Croke versus the Abbott of St Edmunsbury in 1287. Heavy armour was worn, and it seems to have been the practice to halt the contest after one combatant was wounded. However, how many subsequently died of their wounds is unknown.

Whereas on the continent trial by battle endured until the sixteenth century, it had been steadily declining in England since 1300. Battle was uncertain and champions were understandably expensive. Furthermore, it was subject to a number of excuses or 'essoins' that one could offer in order to delay combat. These included the right to defer the contest while one went on crusade, or until one had a male heir of an age to inherit. Battles could be delayed for years. Add to this the hostility of the king and the availability of the comparatively speedy jury trial and one can understand why, as a legal remedy, battle simply withered away.

A fanciful depiction of the clash between Robert de Bruce and Sir Henry de Bohun before the battle of Bannockburn. James Doyle in *A Chronicle of England*, (1864).

The decline of formal trial by battle did not mean the end of other forms of combat. Both contests of chivalry and encounters in tournaments provided opportunities for the demonstration of prowess. In the chivalric duel there was some particular point to prove and intentional killing was permitted. Such an encounter occurred before the battle of Bannockburn in 1314, when Henry de Bohun, an English knight, spotted the Scottish king, Robert Bruce, ahead of his army. Bruce was not armoured but he did not retreat when de Bohun challenged and charged. At the last moment he avoided de Bohun's lance and split the Englishman's head in two with his battle-axe. The fight is said to have raised Scottish morale and to have been something of a metaphor for the battle itself wherein a much smaller but more agile Scottish force defeated the cumbersome English. Anglo–Scottish rivalry was once more the theme of a combat authorised by Richard II in 1390 after an Englishman, Lord Welles

Nicholas Clifford jousts with a French knight in 1381, depicted in an edition of Jean Froissart's chronicle.

and a Scot, Sir David de Lindsay, declared that their respective nations possessed the superior valour. The contest took place on Old London Bridge; Lord Welles was knocked from his horse, but Sir David granted him mercy.

Tournaments began as indiscriminate melees and it is said that in one such affair in 1240, sixty knights were killed. Gradually they evolved into more formal individual contests, where the intention was to win by unhorsing an opponent with a blunted lance. Herein lay the difference in form between tournaments and trials by battle or contests of honour. Once a tournament knight was unhorsed the match was ended, whereas in 'battle' or 'contest' swords, axes or maces would be deployed until one side was decisively defeated. Tournaments, then, were 'sporting' affairs, although that term scarcely conveys the dangers involved, and they were fought as often between enemies or rivals as between friends. This is not to say that personal animosity did not sometimes have its place. In his chronicles, Jean Froissart reported that, in 1381, a group of English knights riding through French territory encountered French knights at an inn. Formally, the parties were at peace, but a French squire, Jean Boucmel, provoked an English squire, Nicholas Clifford, into accepting the offer of 'a tilting match'. Although this was supposed to be a mere test of skill, war lances with sharp points were employed. At the first pass, Clifford's lance bounced off Boucmel's breastplate, snapped and fatally embedded itself in the Frenchman's jugular.

29 June 1559: a lance pierces Henri II's eye during a tournament in the Rue Saint-Antoine, Paris. Lithograph by A. Bayot. (See page 12)

German knights in
single combat; a
wood engraving
after Hans
Burgkmair
(1473–1531).

A tournament
fought with
halberds; woodcut
by Hans Burgkmair
c. 1513.

Tournament knights in Germany, in a coloured woodcut by Hans Schaufelin, Nuremberg, c. 1520.

Although a mere 'sporting' contest, the perils of the joust are apparent. Two German knights jousting, by Schaufelin.

Accident claimed its most famous victim in 1559 when King Henri II o
France was killed during a joust with the captain of his guard, Gabriel, Comt
de Montgomery. The Comte's lance shattered on the helmet of the king an
a splinter went through his eye into his brain. It took him nine days to die.

By the sixteenth century the tournament, like the battle and th
chivalric duel, was in general decline. In England the last duel of chivalr
was fought in 1492, when Sir Hugh Vaughan killed Sir James Parker. As pike
and firearms became more prevalent, knights in cumbersome armour wer
becoming redundant. Furthermore, men ceased to believe that God woul

Armour by Lorenz
Helmschmid of
Ausburg, c. 1520.
Note the plate
protecting the
left shoulder and
neck from the
opponent's lance.
Real Ameria,
Madrid.

make sure that the righteous prevailed. As far back as 1215 the Church, at the Lateran Council, condemned the notion that God would intercede in the petty squabbles of men. Mr Paramour was viewed as eccentric by the court when, in 1571, he proposed a battle over lands in Kent. Elizabeth I intervened to inform the parties that it should be resolved peaceably. The age of mounted personal combat was over, but it had lingered long enough to leave both a romanticised legacy of chivalry and an extremely virile and pugnacious aristocracy, who were soon to prove fully receptive to the new form of contest that was to take its place.

Armour, c. 1600. By this time the plate protecting the left side of the knight had grown. S. R. Meyrick, *Book of Ancient Armour* (1824).

IL CORTEGIANO
DEL CONTE
BALDASSARE
CASTIGLIONE.

Riuedutto, & corretto da ANTONIO
CICCARELLI da Fuligni, Dottore
in Theologia.

Al Serenissimo Signor Duca d'Vrbino.

SIBILLA

IN VENETIA, MDCVI.

Appresso Gioanni Alberti.

THE RENAISSANCE AND THE ARRIVAL OF THE DUEL

FORMAL COMBATS ASIDE, medieval society was inherently violent. The historian Lawrence Stone calculated that, in proportion to the size of the population, there were at least ten times as many murders in medieval England as there are today. Gentlemen routinely carried swords and many of them died as a result of drunken quarrels in taverns. These affrays, in which a man was very likely to be stabbed before he had drawn his sword, were the very opposite of the courteous encounters later described as duels. Duelling was intended as an antidote to indiscriminate killing, owing something to earlier traditions of battle, but due more to a new wave of ideas and manners imported from late Renaissance Italy towards the end of the sixteenth century.

Between 1300 and 1600 Italy produced an astonishing outpouring of art, literature, and philosophy, much of which was prepared to challenge orthodox Christian beliefs. At the same time, noble families within the Italian cities were constantly fighting. In response a system of manners, of courtesy and of civility slowly developed. These were designed to diffuse the tensions between gentlemen. This system, and the literature that supported it, placed great emphasis upon personal honour and reputation. Where a gentleman was insulted, he had a duty to respond in a firm but careful manner. An appropriate apology might be accepted, but if none was forthcoming then a gentleman must challenge the offender. An element of compulsion was involved insofar as a gentleman who failed to respond appropriately to an insult would find himself shunned by society. The code of honour, upon which courtesy was based, authorised a certain type of violence but nonetheless, in the context of the time, it marked an advance in social behaviour. Italian blood feuds continued for generations, sometimes long after the original rights and wrongs were forgotten. Duelling apologists abhorred the blood feud and now insisted that a single, formal and decisive encounter between the principal parties should end the matter once and for all. It was impossible to banish violence from gentlemanly society, apologists argued, but through the mechanism of the duel it could at least be contained.

Opposite:
The frontispiece of Baldassare Castiiglione's *Book of the Courtier*, probably the most important book on chivalry.

The adoption of the rapier (in this example French) led to deep, penetrating wounds that were often fatal.

This new code of honou was first brought back t England by aristocrats and militar officers who had travelled to Italy in th second half of the sixteenth century. With it cam influential books on courtesy, among which wer Girolamo Muzio's *Il Duello*, (Venice, 1550) and mor importantly Castiglione's *Libro del Cortegiano* (*Book of the Courtie* 1528; English, translation 1561). English authors soon followed sui with such books as Simon Robson's *The Courte of Ciuill Courtesie* (1577 and a little later came specific books on duelling, such as George Silver *Paradoxes of Defence* (1599) and John Selden's *The Duello or Single Comb* (1610).

In 1569 an Italian fencing master, Rocco Bonetti, arrived in London ar founded a fencing school at Blackfriars. Others followed, teaching a mor aggressive fencing style than that advocated by English instructors. Th English broadsword was best suited to sweeping blows, the edges slicing th opponent but rarely inflicting fatal wounds; English fencing had evolve accordingly. The Italians, however, favoured the rapier with its lethal poin

talian fencing involved a series of parries and lunges, during which if a point onnected it tended to inflict a small but very deep wound that was often atal. The English fought back against the Italians and in 1587 Austin Bagger ought out and killed Bonetti in a duel; however, the prestige of the Italians vas undiminished. In 1589 Vincento Saviolo arrived and many of his students vere young lawyers who fenced while studying at the Inns of Court. Saviolo imself published a manual of his techniques, *Saviolo His Practise* (1595), while George Silver countered by protesting in his *Paradoxes of Defence* that the ggressive continental systems led to more fatalities.

A duellist had not only to calculate the risk of harm in the duel but also he risk of reprisals afterwards. Nobles were dependent upon the sovereign or their places at court and furthermore duelling was, and was to remain, inlawful. Duelling was extremely rare during Elizabeth I's reign and she ctively intervened in 1597 to prevent duels at court between the Earl of southampton and Lord Grey and between Southampton again and the Earl of Northumberland. However, the number of encounters increased during he reign of James I. There were at least thirty-three duels among the nobility between 1610 and 1629 and there were probably many more that went inreported. Not that James encouraged duelling. On the contrary, at first he acted igorously against it, and between 1602 and 625 his Court of Star Chamber prosecuted round two hundred gentlemen for issuing hallenges to fight duels. An anti-duelling ampaign began, inspired by James and eceiving impetus from a scandalous murder in 612.

The story had begun some seven years efore when a Scottish nobleman, Lord anquhar, had challenged a fencing instructor, 1r Turner, to a match. During the contest urner had put out one of Sanquhar's eyes. The njury had been accidental and so Sanquhar had first forgiven his opponent. Later Sanquhar ravelled to Italy and France. In France he met lenri IV and the king asked how his injury had ome about. Sanquhar explained the ircumstances, whereupon the King replied, Doth the man live?' According to the editor of e *State Trials*, 'That question gave an end to the iscourse but was the beginner of a strange onfusion in his working fancy, which neither

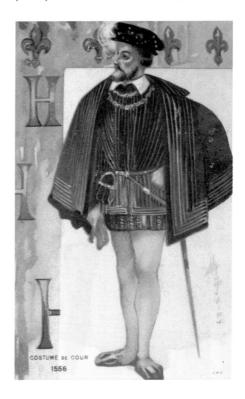

COSTUME DE COUR
1556

Opposite, bottom: English Gentlemen of the fifteenth century. Swords were worn as a matter of course and were readily resorted to in the affrays of the time. Joseph Strutt, *Dress and habits of the people of England* (1796–9).

An English aristocrat in court dress, c. 1556. Such men were ready recipients of the Renaissance ideals arriving from Italy.

Sir Francis Bacon (1561–1626), who led James I's campaign against duelling. Painting by C.W. Quinnell.

time nor distance could compose.' The king's remarks had made Sanquhar deeply ashamed that he had not avenged his injury. It would have been impossible to fence with one eye, so Sanquhar hired two assassins to kill Turner in his house at Blackheath; the men were captured and confessed all.

Sanquhar was tried in Westminster Hall in a case that highlighted the tension between the new values of Renaissance honour and the older ideals of Christian forgiveness and charity. Sanquhar admitted his guilt but argued in effect that it had been less personally dishonourable for him to have had Turner murdered than it would have been to have allowed the injury to go unavenged. 'I considered not my wrongs upon terms of Christianity, for then I should have sought for other satisfaction, but being trained up in the courts of princes and in arms, I stood upon the terms of honour.' Sir Francis Bacon, prosecuting for the king, rejected the foreign notion of honour to which Sanquhar had appealed: 'I must tell you plainly that I conceive you have sucked those affections of dwelling in malice rather out of Italy, and outlandish manners, where you have conversed, than out of any part of this island of England and Scotland.' The jury concurred with Bacon and on 26 June 1612 Sanquhar was hanged outside Westminster Hall.

If the execution was intended as a lesson it had only limited effect. The next year a sensational duel occurred between Edward Sackville and Lord Bruce of Kinloss. They had quarrelled in early 1613, when James I had intervened to prevent a duel; it appeared that the matter had been settled but the parties had been biding their time. They arranged to fight near Antwerp. The encounter itself in the summer of 1613 was a messy affair, fought ankle deep in a water meadow with the parties hacking away until both were wounded, Bruce mortally so.

The will of the King had been flouted and James was spurred to action. Recognising that duellists craved fame, in October 1613 he issued 'a proclamation prohibiting the publishing of any reports or writings of duels'. A second proclamation followed in February 1614 'against private challenge and combats', accompanied by a published treatise by the Earl of Northampton, *A publication of his majesty's edict, and severe censure against priuate combats and combatants*. In the meantime Sir Francis Bacon, as Solicitor

General, declared that the Star Chamber would prosecute anyone who challenged another or who went abroad to fight. In early 1614 he laid specimen charges against minor gentlemen. These attempts were perhaps somewhat belated, for the values of Renaissance honour and courtesy had by now been spreading through the English nobility for more than a generation. However, James had the power of patronage and of the law behind him and his position seemed strong. The question was, how far would he really go to suppress duelling?

An English gentleman in 1588 still bearing a shield to accompany formal attire.

Seventeenth-century English gentlemen duelling using broadswords. J. Strutt, *Dress & Habits of the English people*, (1796–9).

THE SWORD TRIUMPHANT

T SOON BECAME APPARENT that notwithstanding all his speeches and proclamations, James I did not really have the determination to vanquish duelling. Some monarchs in Europe did so: Gustavus Adolphus of Sweden 1594–1632) is said to have abolished military duelling by making the arties fight in front of the army and then executing any survivors. James vas no Adolphus and his position at home was fragile – he depended upon he support of the nobility as much as they depended upon him. He ardoned friends because of his affection for them and enemies because e was afraid of seeming unduly partial. No action was taken against dward Sackville. James in fact set the pattern for all the subsequent nonarchs up to and including Victoria, insofar as they often publicly eplored duelling but found themselves intervening to pardon duellists onvicted by the courts.

Privately, and sometimes not so privately, monarchs often admired uellists and even promoted them. Thomas Hobbes noted in his *Leviathan* 1651) that this posed something of a dilemma for law-abiding gentlemen. lthough 'the Law condemneth Duells; the punishment is made capitall, et, on the other; he that refuseth Duell, is subject to contempt and scorne, vithout remedy; and sometimes by the Sovereign himself thought nworthy to have any charge, or preferment in Warre.' The judges took ieir lead from the king. Because of the premeditation involved, killing in ie course of a planned duel was murder and a capital offence. Yet where ie duel had been fairly conducted sympathetic judges often laboured to nd defects in the evidence and even perverted the law in directing juries) acquit.

When Charles I came to the throne in 1625 he did no better than his ither. With the outbreak of the English Civil War (1642–51), the Puritans n the parliamentary side tried to act. The parliamentary *Articles of War* pecified that 'No Corporal, or other Officer commanding the Watch, shall villingly suffer a Soldier to go forth to a Duel or private Fight upon paine of eath'. Furthermore, a Commons committee set up in 1651 proposed that

Opposite:
A sword duel,
c. 1790. By this
time seconds and
surgeons were
attending on the
field to arrange
the combat and to
attempt to repair
its consequences.
Engraving by
George
Cruikshank.

duellists should lose their right hand and be banished. Although honour culture smacked of vanity and impiety to the Puritans, many on the parliamentary side were gentlemen thoroughly inculcated with its values. During his leadership of the Commonwealth in 1654, Oliver Cromwell had to issue a proclamation ordering imprisonment for six months for anyone sending, delivering or accepting a challenge. This did not prevent the Earl of Chesterfield from wounding John Whalley in 1658 and later being imprisoned to prevent a duel with Lord St John.

The Restoration of the Monarchy in 1660 brought about the reopening of the theatres and the return of aristocratic exiles and their wild drinking which ensured a plentiful supply of quarrels. There were at least 196 duels between 1660 and 1685 with some seventy-five fatalities. In 1666 Sir Edward

Royalist gentlemen of the Civil War period, notorious for their drinking, gambling and quarrelling. Illustration from 'Munchener Bilderbogen' in *Zur Geschichte Der Costume.*

hurlow introduced a bill proposing life imprisonment for duellists. Protests ensured that the bill was diverted to a parliamentary committee where, in time-honoured fashion, it quietly died.

The year 1668 saw another memorable encounter. The Earl of Shrewsbury challenged the Duke of Buckingham, who had been having an affair with Shrewsbury's wife. The two men each appointed a second and all four drew swords in a desperate duel. One second, Sir John Jenkins, was killed outright and Shrewsbury himself died from his wounds two months later. Scandalously, Shrewsbury's widow promptly moved in with Buckingham, who in his turn evicted his own wife. Charles II, who was to issue several proclamations against duelling, promptly pardoned all the surviving parties.

Charles's successors followed in a similar vein. In 1685 James II ordered the lord justices in Ireland to cashier all officers involved in duels, but in the following year he reversed a decree of outlawry on Mr David Lanier, who had killed Sir William Throckmorton. The Glorious Revolution of 1688 brought no change in policy and in 1697 William III pardoned a duellist, William Drummond, after an Edinburgh duel that resulted in two fatalities. Small wonder, then, that as the eighteenth century began, the number of duels appeared to be increasing. In 1712 came the celebrated duel between Charles, the 4th Baron Mohun, and the Duke of Hamilton.

The causes of the duel were in part political. Hamilton was a high Tory who had remained loyal to James II after the Glorious Revolution. Mohun was a Whig and therefore a supporter of the Hanoverian monarchy. They were also engaged in a complex property dispute being fought through the courts with great animosity. Fear that he would lose in court and anger that the new Tory government was seeking peace with France caused Mohun to challenge in November 1712. Hamilton selected a kinsman, Colonel Hamilton, as his second; Mohun chose General George Maccartney. The parties met in Hyde Park on 12 November 1712. The duke's second, Colonel Hamilton, engaged with Maccartney, while Lord Mohun and the Duke of Hamilton fought. A confused melee resulted, in which both Mohun and the Duke of Hamilton were fatally wounded. The manner of the duke's death became the subject of bitter controversy. When Colonel Hamilton was tried at the Old Bailey he claimed that Maccartney had treacherously stabbed the

Lord Charles Mohun, who was killed in a duel with the Duke of Hamilton in 1712.

duke after he had dropped his sword. He himself was found guilty of mer manslaughter and released. Maccartney, who had escaped to the Lo« Countries, produced a pamphlet in his own defence denying the allegation and a war of words began.

The duel had been conducted upon the cusp of a change in the role of th seconds. Mohun had suggested that the seconds should not fight – althoug in the event they did so. Previously, seconds had been expected to join in, b« during the eighteenth century the duties of the seconds changed so that l the middle of the century it was almost unknown for them actively t participate. Indeed, in many duels fought up until about 1770, there were n seconds at all. Rather, these duels bore not a little resemblance to the earli« affrays. Quarrels, fought after excessive drinking and gambling, resulted i the immediate settlement of disputes. Typical in that respect was the quarr between Major Oneby and Mr Gower in 1726. Both men had been playi cards with others in a tavern when Gower made some jest to which drunken Oneby objected. Words were exchanged, Oneby threw a bottl and Gower replied with a candlestick. The rest of the company intervene and calmed the situation, but when Gower tried to shake hands with Oneb the Major replied, 'No damn you I will have your blood'. Everyone hurried made to leave, but Oneby contemptuously called Gower back. The door w

A depiction of the duel between Lord Mohun and the Duke of Hamilton, purporting to show the latter being treacherously stabbed. Illustration by Phiz (Hablot Knight Browne) in Capt. L. Benson's *Remarkable Trials*, (1872).

barred, swords drawn and Gow« killed. Remarkably, Oneby w subsequently convicted of Gowei murder and he only cheated th hangman by committing suicid However, there had been a numb« of aggravating factors. Oneby ha reacted disproportionately to a inoffensive remark by Gower and h had thereafter refused a genero« apology. Perhaps most important Oneby was an experienc« swordsman, whereas Gower had ha no training whatsoever.

Although the fashion for wearin a sword was very much in declin« still many young gentlem« continued to practise fencing and purchase the elaborate instructi« manuals newly available. Impromp encounters were coming to an e« by the time that the 5th Lord Byr«

and Mr Chaworth fought in a coffee house in Pall Mall in 1765. The context was a public dinner and an argument over whose estates contained the most game. The men withdrew to a side room and Chaworth was killed. Byron was tried before his peers in Westminster Hall but convicted only of manslaughter. He was symbolically branded with a cold iron on his hand and released with a fine.

By 1765 a new species of seconds was emerging. These new seconds, or 'friends' as they were also called, were no mere servants of their patrons, but rather independent gentlemen in their own right. Their function was to act as guardians of the honour of the contending parties and to attempt to resolve the matter peaceably. Where one party had offended another it would have been shameful to make monetary reparation. Instead, a gentleman might make a carefully worded apology, one that did not damage his reputation, and the opposing gentleman would offer a gracious acceptance. One of the duties of the seconds was to publicise both the facts of the dispute and of the resolution, vouchsafing that nothing had been done that sullied either party. Eighteenth- and nineteenth-century newspapers often had advertisements recording the amicable resolution of a dispute, and many more disputes were resolved than ever went so far as a duel – in his honour critique Abraham Bosquett wrote that he had been a second twenty-five times and that 'Life or

A plate from a fencing manual of the late eighteenth century. Thrusts and lunges were aimed at the internal organs.

Escrime, de la riposte de prime, du coupé simple, de la passe en quarte, et de l'echappement du pié gauche en arriere.

honour were never lost in my hands'. However, if all negotiations failed the
it was the seconds who would determine the date, place and circumstance
of the actual encounter. Their role was crystallised by the publication of the
Clonmel Code in 1777, a code supposedly to be followed by all Irish duellists
By this time seconds were expected to manage all aspects of an encounter
However, once the two parties started to slash at each other the degree of
control they could have was limited, so it is probably no coincidence that the
rise in the seconds' authority coincided with the fundamental change
occasioned by the adoption of the pistol.

A photograph
from the 1950s
of Moll's Coffee
House, Plymouth.
Quarrels
in coffee houses
accounted for
a significant
proportion of
the duels in the
seventeenth and
eighteenth century.
From here sea
captains had
headed for their
ships to set sail
against the Armada
in 1588.

PISTOLS AT DAWN: THE CLASSIC ENGLISH DUEL

PISTOLS WERE USED experimentally in a duel in 1711, but the sword remained dominant until the 1770s. There was a brief period of transition when both sword and pistol were used. A single volley of shots followed by the drawing of swords was employed both when Richard Brinsley Sheridan fought Mr Matthews in 1772, and when Captain Stoney fought the Reverend Bate in 1778. However, swords were used only once in the twenty-one duels reported between 1780 and 1789. Significantly, for on the continent the sword was retained as the weapon of choice, this was a duel involving a German officer. The move to the pistol in Britain may have had much to do with a sense of fairness. Swordsmanship required a specialist education that not every gentleman had received. John Cockburn pointed out in his *History and Examination of Duels* (1720) that it was 'Base, for one of the sword to call out another who was never bred to it, but wears it for fashion's sake.' The fashion for wearing swords had declined after 1720 and by 1793 the anonymous *Advice to Seconds* was declaring that the adoption of the pistol was fortunate, since 'every swordsman knows how rarely the parties are of equal skill.' The pistol gave the young less of an advantage over the old and the inaccuracy of smooth-bored weapons meant that there was an element of uncertainty for both parties.

The chances of being killed or wounded depended very much upon the distance at which the seconds decided fire should be exchanged and upon the number of shots that they subsequently permitted. Twelve paces was the most common distance, followed by ten. Twenty paces risked having the affair ridiculed; fewer than ten and the chance of a fatality increased dramatically. When Lieutenant W. and Captain I. met in 1803, the distance set was only six paces and the result was a rare instance where both parties were killed instantaneously. Unlike the practice sometimes employed on the continent, where men stood back to back, paced, then turned and fired, in Britain the seconds marked out the distance and placed the parties on their respective spots. It should be said that there was no formal system which dictated the number of shots which might be exchanged, nor did English

Gentlemen equipped with protective masks fencing in St James's Street in 1821. Swordplay in England had become a mere recreational activity as the pistol had long supplanted the sword as the weapon of choice for duelling. Coloured engraving by I. R. & G. Cruikshank, in Pierce Egan's *Life in London* (1821).

gentlemen declare theatrically that the fight would be, 'To the death!' The shots exchanged depended upon the courage of the parties, the depth of their animosities, and the determination of the seconds and so on. Broadly though, it can be observed that the duels were particularly likely to be fought up until the point of death or serious injury when they involved contests over women. However, it was also the case that in the final decades of the duel, the number of shots exchanged declined as gentlemen increasingly felt that a single exchange, or sometimes the firing of a single shot by the party that had been offended, was all that honour required.

A pistol duellist stood side-on to his opponent, pointing his pistol at the ground. On a signal he was expected to raise his arm rigidly in a single movement and to fire immediately without taking careful aim. Firing was thereby made less accurate and standing sideways minimised the target and offered some protection to the vital organs. Generally, the parties fired at the same time. Sometimes they tossed for the right to fire first or first fire was given to the party that had been particularly wronged. It required great nerve to stand still while being fired at by a party that was under no immediate threat themselves. Whatever the method employed, duelling in Britain was extremely dangerous. Casualty lists are incomplete but the 834 duels I have surveyed between 1785 and 1844 resulted in 277 fatalities and 341 wounded – a death and an injury rate of about 17 per cent and 20 per cent respectively. Who, then, were the gentlemen involved and what quarrels led them to hazard death or the horrors of surgery and amputation?

In the 1830s about one third of all duellists either held or had held military commissions. Earlier during the Napoleonic Wars this figure was as high as two thirds. These officers and also the colonial administrators carried the duel out into all corners of the empire and the former were much the largest single group of duellists. They had to be prepared to defend their honour and, by extension, that of their ship or regiment, or else suffer the scorn of their fellows. In 1783 Mr Cunningham refused to accept a challenge from Mr Riddell after a quarrel at cards. The officers of Cunningham's regiment told him he would be forced to resign if he did not fight. Reluctantly Cunningham agreed; he killed his opponent but was himself severely injured. In 1785 Captain Bulkley of the Guards received an insulting letter from Captain Brisco. Foolishly he made an official complaint, whereupon the officers decided that no one would speak to him until he had duelled like a gentleman. Unofficial sanctions aside, the Articles of War contained a provision known as the 'Devil's Article' whereby an officer who had behaved 'in a scandalous infamous manner' could be cashiered. Sometimes this was employed against officers who had declined challenges. In 1776, a Captain Beilby was court-martialled in Minorca for having received 'language unbecoming the character of an officer and a gentleman without taking proper notice of it.' It bears repeating that duelling was illegal and that in effect officers were being punished for refusing to break the law.

Breaking the law did not necessarily deter even the lawyers. Lord Norbury, Chief Justice of the Common Pleas, said of himself that he began the world with fifty pounds and a pair of hair-trigger pistols. Jonah Barrington, King's Counsel in Ireland, claimed in his memoirs that 'In my time, the

Below left: Pistol shooting in 1844 – note the stiff upright posture, with one arm tucked behind the back and the leading arm almost fully extended.

Below: Another view from 1844. The marksman stands sideways; in a duel this and the leading arm would offer some protection to the organs. Both images from D'Houdetot, *Le tir au pistolet*, (1844).

umber of killed and wounded among the bar was very considerable. The
ther learned professions suffered much less.' A fashion for lawyerly duelling
eems to have swept right across the common-law world in the final decades
f the eighteenth century. In America perhaps as many as 90 per cent of the
uellists in the southern states at this time were attorneys. In 1801 Tennessee
orced entrants to the bar to take an oath against duelling. At the trial in Upper
anada in 1819 of Richard Uniacke Junior for killing William Bowie, almost
ue entire bar of the province were either implicated in the duel or came
orward to act as character witnesses. In England, with the exception of Lord
ldon, who duelled while Solicitor General, most lawyerly duellists were
om the lower ranks of the profession. After 1820 their numbers declined
ad the mantle was taken up by the doctors. What both the doctors and the
wyers had in common was that they had to struggle to be regarded as
entlemen and representing themselves as men of honour helped them to
ccomplish this. The doctors were somewhat tardy and appeared as
ombatants in the final decades of duelling. The very last duel reported in
cotland was between two medical students in 1842 and earlier that year a
octor and a surgeon were reported by *The Times* as having duelled following
dispute about credit for an anatomical discovery. The paper did not report

Opposite: A set of
nineteenth-century
smooth-bore
duelling pistols.

Warren Hastings,
first Governor-
General of India,
wounds Sir Philip
Francis in a
duel in 1780.
A. D. M'Cormick in
V. Surridge, *India*
(1909).

Lord Eldon, who duelled while solicitor general.

whether each hoped to demonstrate their discovery upon the cadaver of the other.

Officers aside, the next most numerous species of duellist were actually not the professional men, but rather the aristocratic rakes of Georgian London. Such men were obsessively concerned with the regard of others. They dressed in the latest fashions, ridiculed those who did not, and paraded in Hyde Park to be seen by all. The casual elegance of such men belied their extreme physicality, for such men had been educated in the almost bestial atmosphere of pre-reform public schools. Respectable society was shocked by their membership of the Infidel and Hellfire clubs and by their smashing of lamps, breaking windows and attacking the night watch for sport.

Notwithstanding their polished exterior, English gentlemen enjoyed their violent recreations. Three gentlemen attack two men of the watch. Print by T. Lane, published by Humphrey (1822).

The cream of fashionable society enjoy a dance at Almack's in 1821. Drawn and engraved by R. & G. Cruikshank in Pierce Egan's *Life in London* (1821).

Rakes had a vigorous life on the street, but during the second half of the eighteenth century private clubs were emerging which offered gentlemen an escape from the 'hurly burly' of the city and enabled them to relax with men of their own class. Perhaps the most important of these was Almack's, established in 1764. Almack's later became particularly renowned for its elegant balls and being a member of or excluded from Almack's placed a marker upon one's position in society.

If Almack's offered a variety of civilised entertainments, it nevertheless began life as a gambling club. Immense fortunes were won and lost in a single night there. Charles James Fox, the Whig politician, and his brother, Stephen, were said to have lost over £32,000 there over the course of just three days — well over a million pounds in today's money. Gambling declined somewhat with the onset of the nineteenth century: cockfighting and prizefighting had become a lot less popular by the 1820s, though horseracing remained very important. Men were still being ruined at the card tables and the careful decorum of the players was liable to break down at any suggestion of misconduct.

Yet it was not loss of money, but loss of dignity that men most feared. Gentlemen were at their most aggressive when hoping to impress women. This has to be qualified by the observation that, although romantic chivalry and the values of honour culture are often confused, gentlemen very rarely intervened to protect women over whom they had no control or in whom they had no interest. One did not intervene if one's neighbour beat his wife, but one might react aggressively if one had taken a woman to the theatre and she was inconvenienced. In the first instance a gentleman's own honour was

Right: Those who
did not dance
amused themselves
by playing cards.
Drawn and
engraved by I. R.
& G. Cruikshank in
Pierce Egan's *Life in
London* (1821).

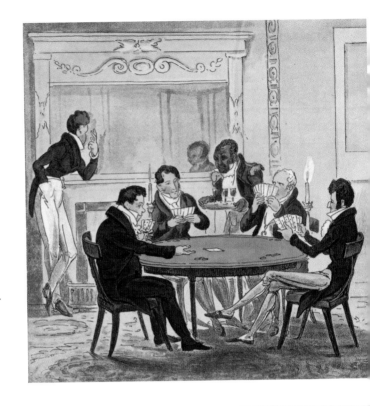

Below: In the
1820s, disputes at
the gaming or card
tables were liable
to lead to fisticuffs.
Aquatint by
E. Duncan after
H. Alken & T. J.
Rawlins: Nimrod's
*Memoirs of the Life
of John Mytton*
(1837).

...ot engaged and nobody thought ill of him if he did not intervene. In the second case, the inconvenience was to the woman, but the implication was that her escort was unable to protect her. Society, in short, was divided into zones of male interest over women and when those zones were violated men conventionally defended their own honour by reference to the interests of the women themselves. Thus three or four duels were occasioned in 1773 by a group of men ogling a Mrs Hartley while she was being dined by the Reverend Bate (see also pages 27 and 42). In 1812, a duel was fought after a latecomer attempted to squeeze down a row past some ladies to take his theatre seat. In 1840 a particularly unfortunate duel was occasioned by Captain Fleetwood's dog. It had been swimming in the Serpentine in Hyde Park and, upon emerging, shook itself vigorously over the dresses of two young women out walking with Mr Brocksopp.

Walks in the park aside, conventionally the place one took a lady one wished to court was to the theatre and this perhaps explains why men were very much on their honour there and why theatres have a disproportionate place in the history of duelling. In 1761 Colonel Grey was killed and Major Egerton wounded after Grey had bumped into Egerton while leaving a performance. Egerton had called Grey 'a stupid booby', blows had been exchanged and a duel had become inevitable. There were at least six duels caused by disputes at the theatre between 1793 and 1796 alone. For example, in 1796 Major Sweetman was killed after having stepped on the toe of Captain Watson.

Many women seem to have been attracted to duellists. In 1763 the radical politician John Wilkes was seriously wounded by Samuel Martin, a supporter

The Drury Lane theatre in 1820. Of all public engagements it seems that a trip to the theatre was the one that was most likely to lead to a challenge and a duel. Thomas Rowlandson, *The Second Tour of Doctor Syntax* (1798).

Overleaf:
A fashionable duel of the 1820s. The combatants fire upon the dropping of a handkerchief; their up-to-the-minute attire includes pleated and 'Cossack' trousers, coats with roll collars, top hats and a braided blue coat. Unnamed artist, possibly Robert Cruikshank.

John Wilkes (1725–97). Wilkes found that duelling not only enhanced his political reputation but also secured the affections of the opposite sex.

The extraordinary Thomas Pitt, 2nd Baron Camelford (1775–1804), a great-nephew of Pitt the Elder. Engraving by an unnamed artist in Kirby's *Wonderful Museum* (1805).

of George III. The affair was no without some benefits however. H later wrote to his friend Charle Churchill 'A sweet girl, whom I hav sighed for unsuccessfully these fou months, now tells me she will trus her honour to a man who takes s much care of his own.' In some case fighting a duel seems to have been necessary precursor to marriage almost as if the bride or her famil were testing the mettle of the suito In 1772 Richard Brinsley Sherida fought a desperate duel with a riva before securing Miss Linley. In 177 Captain Stoney became engaged t Lady Strathmore after having fough the editor of the *Morning Post* who ha published derogatory remarks abou her. In 1811 Mr Wellesley-Pole fough a rival suitor, Lord Kilworth, and late married Miss Tylney Long.

Women were not necessaril helpless innocents and in some case they exploited honour culture fo their own ends. In no case was thi more clearly demonstrated than in th events that led up to the death o Thomas Pitt, 2nd Baron Camelford, i 1804. Camelford was one of the mos outrageous, colourful and fearsom men of his age. During naval servic he killed a fellow officer in a disput over seniority and assaulted his forme captain in London. Discharged int civilian life, he thereafter passed hi time in violence, designing ingeniou weapons and travelling to France t try to assassinate members of th French government. Small wonde that his biographer, Nikolai Tolstoy called him 'The Half-Mad Lord'

1804, however, he fell foul of Fanny Simmonds. Simmonds had been the lover of one of Camelford's friends, Captain Best. In 1801 she left Best for Camelford, although all three seem to have remained friends. In March 1804 he went to Camelford and alleged that Best had insulted her at the opera. Camelford challenged Best but subsequently discovered that her story was false. However, the duel went ahead because Best was renowned as a marksman and Camelford was afraid that others might think him a coward he withdrew. Best neatly shot Camelford dead at the first exchange of fire. Simmonds's motives are unclear, but Tolstoy notes some evidence that he might have been in the employ of the French government.

Men such as Camelford, who were ever ready to be insulted and to respond with violence, were looked upon by some as social monsters and avoided. However, reputations such as his were not without utility. While they lived, such men were rarely contradicted, others were deferential to them and rushed to do their bidding and, in a virile society, while they were feared, they were also admired by men and women alike. In her letters, Hester Stanhope recalled the effect Camelford could have upon a mixed company: she remembered, 'His taking me one evening to a party, and it was quite a scene to notice how the men shuffled away, and the women stared at him.'

The Caneing in Conduit Street, Dedicated to the Flag Officers of the British Navy, 1796, by James Gillray (1757–1815). Lord Camelford attacks his former Captain George Vancouver. 'Draw your sword, Coward! What you won't? Why then take that, Lubber! And that … And that … And that!' Vancouver cries for help, 'Murder! Murder! Watch! Constable! Keep him off brother, while I run to my Lord Chancellor for protection. Murder! Murder! Murder!'

THE EXTINCTION OF ENGLISH HONOUR

A T THE OUTSET of the nineteenth century it must have seemed that duelling was firmly entrenched in English society. The centre of activity as London, where off-duty officers spent their leave, where gentlemen aunted themselves and where aspiring professionals headed to make their reers. About half the duels in England and Wales between 1780 and 1845 ere fought in London or within a day's ride (gentlemen often rode outside e city to shoot each other). Elsewhere, clusters of duels could be observed ound garrison towns and major military ports. They were also to be found racecourses such as Ascot, Chester, and Nantwich. For example, in 1784 quarrel erupted at Ascot between Mr England and Mr Rowls after England, ho was owed money, urged gentlemen not to bet with Rowls as he did not ay his debts. Rowls was killed in the subsequent duel.

There were also some duels being fought among the landed squires thinly istributed throughout the countryside. Even more than politics, the redominant cause of quarrels seems to have been the English obsession with unting. Disputes over trespassing, over the rearing of game and the reservation of foxes often occurred. In 1759 the Earl of Leicester instructed s game-keeper to kill all the foxes on his land to preserve his game birds, ut he was promptly challenged by George Townshend from the local fox int. Mr Warden was killed in 1792 after confronting Mr Bond, who was respassing on his land. Mr Tythen died in 1806 following a quarrel between ooting parties in Buckinghamshire and when Thomas Ritchie tried to order shooting party off his father's estates in 1818 he was assaulted and allenged.

Scandalous duels were the very stuff of which newspaper circulations ere made and they were much publicised and discussed. Yet it is easy to in a false impression from newspapers and romantic memoirs. There were any gentlemen who had never been attracted to honour culture and in the ineteenth century the importance of such men was growing. In many towns elling was actually very rare. When the *Hereford Times* reported a duel in recon in 1837 it declared that 'It has caused a great sensation in this town,

Opposite:
The aftermath of a duel, c. 1833. A duellist was expected to show solicitude for his fallen opponent and to procure him medical attention. A series of duels in the 1840s in which wounded gentlemen were abandoned on the field did much to discredit duelling. *The Life of a Nobleman*, unnamed artist, published by G. Davis.

such a circumstance not having occurred for a great number of years.' Below the level of titled gentlemen, the countryside was filled with a solid core of farmers who had never adopted duelling. In 1810 for example, regiment officers at Bletchingley in West Sussex tried in vain to provoke the local farmers to duel. The cause was once more hunting. The officers had behaved in an unruly fashion on the farmers' lands and had been banned. The officers then turned up at a town meeting and tried to provoke the farmers' leader Mr Hitchin, into a duel with the regiment's colonel. Hitchin replied calmly that he had a family, that he had nothing to do with pistols, but that he was happy to meet the colonel with his horsewhip. He then prosecuted the colonel at the West Sussex assizes. Hitchin and his supporters were men of substance, most likely more prosperous than the officers, but they did not feel the appeal of honour culture.

Furthermore, while regional newspapers reported some duels in the older coastal towns such as Liverpool, Norwich, Bristol and Plymouth, there were hardly any duels in the manufacturing towns. Manchester scarcely figures at all in duelling reports; nor do Birmingham, Leeds or Sheffield. The hard-headed practical men who ran these cities had little time for Romantic honour. They were men of science who calculated things, took the long view and scorned the drinking, gambling and whoring that characterised the life of the London rake. The influence of such men grew along with the manufacturing cities in the first half of the nineteenth century. Manchester for example, had a population of only 70,000 in 1801, but by 1831 this had

The Reverend Sir Henry Bate Dudley (1745–1824), whose status as a man of the cloth did not prevent him being one of the most avid duellists of the late eighteenth century.

Bate Dudley.

grown to 142,000. The reasons for the final demise of duelling in Britain are somewhat controversial but all commentators agree that the development of a new middle class who were increasingly politically important after the 1832 Reform Act, had much to do with it.

Middle-class men not only ascended the social ladder themselves; they also influenced those above them. By 1837, when Victoria came to the throne, there was a new type of gentleman in society: abstemious, hard-working and pious. For a long time the Anglican Church did very little to prevent duelling and ministers thought themselves gentlemen, sometimes duelling themselves. Most notoriously, the Reverend Sir Henry Bate Dudley (1745–1824) earned the nickname 'the fighting parson', having fought at least two duels and in 1781 the Reverend Allen killed a Lieutenant Dulany in a dispute over the War of Independence. However, religious revival began in the eighteenth century, notably in Wales, with the work of the Methodists George Whitfield and John Wesley and by the early nineteenth century, Evangelicals, Methodists, Quakers and other religious groups were exerting a powerful influence on society; they were particularly important in the campaign against slavery. By the 1820s even Anglican vicars were preaching about the evils of duelling and finding that there was a growing constituency firmly against it.

For a time some carried on oblivious and in 1829 a momentous duel occurred when the Duke of Wellington and Lord Winchilsea met on Battersea Fields. The cause of the duel was a dispute over the foundation of King's College London. Both men supported King's, which was intended to be an Anglican rival to the secular University College founded in 1826. Wellington was then serving as Prime Minister and in order to quell unrest in Ireland he found himself obliged to support an act for the emancipation of Catholics, the Catholic Relief Act 1829. Winchilsea was a man of profoundly anti-Catholic sentiments and so published a letter noting the hypocrisy of Wellington in promoting an Anglican college while at the same time seeking to change the constitution. Wellington challenged and fired a

The duel between the Duke of Wellington and Lord Winchilsea in 1829. Winchilsea did not fire back at the duke and by this time single-shot duels were becoming common. Engraving by W. B. Waller.

single shot at Winchilsea's legs on 14 March; Winchilsea in return fired into the air. Great disquiet resulted, for in 1829 the country was troubled by internal disorder and many wondered what would have happened had Winchilsea fired back and killed the man who was holding the government together. In such times, abolitionists argued, duelling was a weak and foolish indulgence. They noted that the government was struggling to get the labouring classes to obey the law; how, then, could the titled act as though they were above it?

A scandal in 1840 also made the point. In 1837 Lord Cardigan was appointed to the 11th Light Dragoons. His behaviour was so arrogant that nineteen subordinate officers left the regiment. The radical press made much of his high-handed conduct and in 1839 he challenged the editor of the *Morning Herald*. In 1840 he was criticised in the press by one of his former officers, Captain Harvey Tuckett, and in response the two men fought on Wimbledon Common. Tuckett was wounded and Wandsworth magistrates charged Cardigan under an 1837 act, whereby wounding with intent to commit murder was a capital offence. Cardigan was tried before his peers in Westminster Hall, but he was acquitted upon a technicality. The prosecution neglected to call Captain Tuckett into court and relied upon the Captain's card to prove his identity. The card identified him as 'Harvey Tuckett' whereas the indictment against Cardigan had specified his opponent as 'Harvey Garnett Phipps Tuckett'. This minor technicality was enough to cause the Lords to acquit, but the verdict was greeted with outrage and cynicism and not just in the radical press. Even *The Times* condemned Cardigan and argued that he should have been treated like any common felon. By 1840 the stock of duellists was very low indeed.

Two further scandalous duels followed. To general horror, in July 1843 Lieutenant Munro killed his own brother-in-law, Colonel Fawcett, following a quarrel between Munro and his sister. With the exception of just one of the seconds, none of the surviving participants behaved like gentlemen; all abandoned the deceased on the field and refused to submit to justice. Then in 1845, Mr Hawkey shot down Mr Seton in response to Seton's alleged advances to his wife. What offended the public was the fact that Hawkey had shown no solicitude to the fallen Seton, merely remarking immediately to his second, 'I am off to France.' Eventually he surrendered himself and stood trial in July 1846 at Winchester Assizes. He was acquitted, but *The Times* fulminated that 'There was evidence to convict twenty murderers, and not an attempt was made to disprove a tittle of it.'

The number of men duelling by the 1840s was very small. Lord Hardinge, Secretary at War, made an important stand against it when, in February 1844, he refused a pension to Colonel Fawcett's widow. No widow of a duellist would henceforth receive a pension and the army would dismiss

ny man who had challenged another. For the first time there was a sense that
he government really meant it and henceforth officers routinely declined
hallenges on the basis of the detrimental effect it would have upon their
amily and their careers. Without the support of the officer corps, duelling
imply ceased. The very last encounter was fought in October 1852 at
nglefield Green in Surrey and was between two Frenchmen; Monsieur
mmanuel Barthelemy and Lieutenant Frederic Cornet. Cornet was killed,
arthelemy fled, and three of the seconds were imprisoned for manslaughter.

James Brudenell,
the 7th Earl of
Cardigan (1797–
1868).

Le Petit Journal

SUPPLÉMENT ILLUSTRÉ
Huit pages : CINQ centimes

TOUS LES JOURS
Le Petit Journal
5 Centimes

TOUS LES VENDREDIS
Le Supplément illustré
5 Centimes

Quatrième Année — SAMEDI 7 JANVIER 1893 — Numéro

LE DUEL DÉROULÈDE - CLÉMENCEAU

THE EUROPEAN TWILIGHT

T HAT FRENCHMEN should duel in England was somewhat ironic, for historically it was in France where the culture of honour was most firmly rooted. Duelling culture arrived in the sixteenth century as a consequence of French campaigns in Italy and it arrived at a time when battle still remained a recognised procedure. Thus the transition from one to the other had been fairly easy. Battle as a formal affair came to an end with a spectacular encounter between Guy Chabot, Baron de Jarnac and François de Vivonne, Seigneur de la Châtaigneraye on 10 July 1547.

The cause seems to have been a rumour spread by the Dauphin (crown prince) that Jarnac was having an affair with his stepmother. The prince's position was unassailable but when a courtier, La Châtaigneraie, repeated the tale, Jarnac demanded a battle to restore his reputation. François I refused permission, but then he died and the Dauphin, now Henri II, authorised the contest. On the day the men fought with shield and long sword and the expectation was that the experienced swordsman La Châtaigneraye would prevail. However, he was defeated by a slicing blow that severed the tendons behind his left knee, a blow known thereafter as a 'coup de Jarnac'.

La Châtaigneraye later died from his wounds and Henri II's role in the affair discredited judicial combat. Duelling, however, was by then an established feature of life among the French nobility. In England duelling deaths were numbered in the dozens, but between 1588 and 1608 some seven to eight thousand French noblemen died in such contests. Louis XIII issued an edict against duelling in 1626 and in 1627 the Comte de Bouteville, an habitual duellist, was executed for having dared to fight a duel in the Place Royale. Louis, like James I of England, protected his favourites and pardoned many duellists. His successors did no better. The duel continued with vigour into the eighteenth century and in the main it continued with the sword.

In the early nineteenth century duelling came under pressure with the Court of Cassation (supreme court) leading a vigorous campaign against it. By 1840 there were only ten fencing halls in France and the duel looked doomed. Yet, surprisingly, it blossomed again and this time as a late child of

Opposite:
A rare pistol duel between Monsieur Déroulède and Monsieur Clemenceau in 1893 – both survived the encounter. Henri Meyer in *Le Petit Journal*, 7 January 1893.

Charles V (1500–
58), Holy Roman
Emperor and
warrior king, did
much to propagate
European honour
culture when
he challenged
Francis I
(1494–1547) of
France to a duel
in 1526. In the
event the duel
never went ahead.
Painting by Titian
(1490–1576) in the
Prado Museum,
Madrid, Spain.

the Revolution. Under the stifling autocracy of Louis Napoleon, bourgeoi
Frenchmen began to regard it as a badge of republican liberty that they to
could fight for their honour. Duelling became, somewhat paradoxically
associated with French democratic sentiments and much the same could be
observed in revolutionary Italy, which was unified after 1852. In both
countries duelling became fashionable among progressive politicians, lawyer
and journalists, all of whom were eager to demonstrate that they were equa
to and as much gentlemen as their better-born rivals.

To no small degree this resurgence of duelling was made possible b
ability to finesse sword encounters in ways that were not possible with

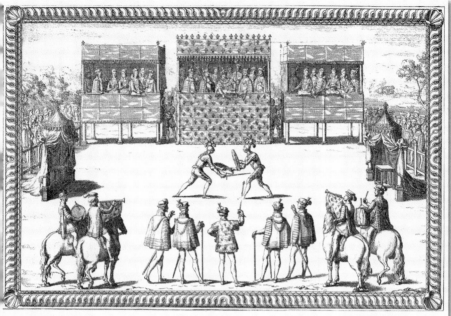

DUEL DE JARNAC ET DE LA CHATEIGNERAIE DEVANT LE ROI, A SAINT-GERMAIN, EN 1547.
(Fac-simile d'une estampe de la Bibliothèque Nationale).

The duel between the Baron de Jarnac and La Châtaigneraye at Saint-Germain, Paris, in 1547.

pistols. Rapiers were replaced by less lethal epées and protective clothing appeared. Encounters could be limited to a number of set passes and combat might be ended at the first sight of blood. In 1898 the then current and the former chiefs of the French secret service, Colonel Henry and Monsieur Picquart, fought one other. Each had given evidence on opposite sides during the trial of Émile Zola for libel. After a few passes Henry sustained a minor wound on the elbow and the seconds interfered to end the affair.

Encounters were still not entirely risk free. In 1895, for example, at Neuilly, Monsieur Le Chatelier fatally stabbed Harry Alis through a lung at the first pass and pistols were still sometimes used where the grievance ran deep. Monsieur Clemenceau (later Prime Minister of France) and Monsieur Déroulède fought just such an encounter in December 1892 after Déroulède had accused Clemenceau of corruption during the building of the Panama Canal. After a single and bloodless exchange of shots, however, the seconds intervened. In general terms it remains correct to say that whereas the English duel remained extremely dangerous right up until the moment that it disappeared, the French and Italian duels continued but grew ever safer. Jacopo Gelli reported that there had been 3,918 duels in Italy between 1879 and 1899 but only about twenty deaths. In later French duels death rates

Monsieur Le
Chatelier kills
Monsieur Harry
Alis in 1895. Tofani
in *Le petit Journal*,
17 March 1895.

were very much less than 1 per cent and in 1880 Mark Twain was able to parody the French duel thus: 'Much as the modern French duel is ridiculed by certain smart people, it is in reality one of the most dangerous institutions of our day. Since it is always fought in the open air, the combatants are nearly sure to catch cold.'

A German commentator described French duels as 'a trivial game', for German duelling was unique insofar as there may have been more fatal duels fought in the second half of the nineteenth century than the first. As elsewhere, the duel had entered the German states from Italy, via the universities of Salerno and Bologna and through the occupation of foreign armies during the Thirty Years' War (1618–48). All German states had legislation prohibiting duelling in the seventeenth and eighteenth centuries but like everywhere else most rulers had been obliged to tolerate it. What marked out the German experience as different was the intensity with which the practice became embedded within the Prussian army and the particular domination that the army enjoyed over Prussian society.

In Prussia a twin-track legal system began to develop whereby those whose social situation made them *satisfaktionsfahig*, capable of giving satisfaction in a duel, were treated quite differently from the general population. In 1843 honour courts within the army were allowed to umpire

uels and after 1874 they had formal powers to dismiss any who refused a
hallenge. Such duels were often fought with pistols and casualty rates were
igh. The historian V. G. Keirnan believes that such duels were tolerated

The Marquis of
Dion and Monsieur
Gerault Richard
duel in November
1902 in Neuilly
Saint James
(France).

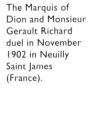

A caricature
entitled, 'Halt
Gentlemen,
Honour is
Satisfied!' in
L'Assiette au Beurre,
26 January 1907.
The merest
scratch ends this
French duel fought
in front of an
enthusiastic
crowd.

because of the frustrations of a highly militarised state engaged in hardly any actual military activity. Germany had very few overseas territories and from the end of the Franco–Prussian War in 1871 until 1914, few officers saw active service. They were bored and deprived of any alternative way of demonstrating their abilities, so they turned to duelling.

If the slaughter of the First World War made and broke many reputations, it certainly broke duelling. The idea of individual honour and studied gentlemanly combat drowned in the horror of the trenches, where industrial war made individual affronts seem of vanishing importance. In none of the European states did duelling recover completely from that war. Honour culture had been confined to a certain class, but it had been international. Nationalism, collective ideologies and whole peoples at war swept duelling aside as an irrelevant

A Prussian officer, c. 1900. Illustration by E. Thony in *Simplicissimus*.

Student duelling societies offered companionship, alcohol and a chance to impress women. Unattributed lithograph, Berlin, 1898.

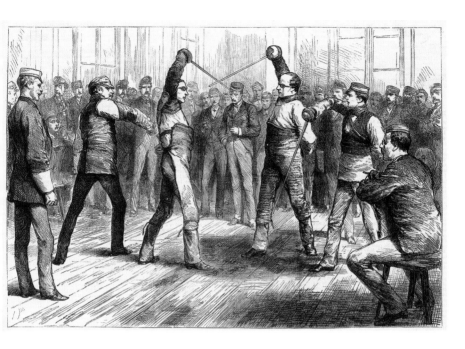

ntiquarianism. Some held on to the old ideals; there were some duels in
Europe in the 1920s and 1930s. However, the Second World War was the final
death knell, save one form of duelling that still survives today and is practised
in some German and Austrian
universities. Founded in the early
nineteenth century, German duelling
fraternities offered students who
could prove their courage the
chance of social advancement and
opportunities for the perennial
student activities of drinking and
chasing women. In the latter, one was
most likely to succeed if one acquired
the kudos of a fine duelling scar. At
first the enterprise was a risky one.
Duels were rough affairs using the
tossdegen, a rapier with a penetrative
power that resulted in many internal
injuries. However, the weapon
was banned in Breslau in 1819 and
in many universities thereafter.

A student duel,
c. 1880. Note the
eye protection and
the formal stylised
positions and
passes of the
combatants.

A doctor attends
to a duellist after
a *Mensur* in 1895.
The student hopes
that he has been
scarred for life.
Georg Muhlberg,
1905.

Preparations for a student fencing match in 1933. The fencer is protected by padding to the chest and the arms, with a high padded collar to guard the throat. He will shortly don goggles – by this time the *Mensur* has become a sport. Illustration by E. Thony in *Simplicissimus*, 1933.

In its place came the *Schläger*, a straight-edged weapon without a point. This sliced flesh but rarely penetrated organs. Further refinements appeared: gloves to protect hands; padding to protect arms and legs; and, after 1857, protective goggles.

By the 1870s three main student duelling associations had emerged and the student duel became a highly formalised affair, a *Mensur*. The aim was not to seriously harm one's opponent but merely to cut him or to be cut in return. The scars sustained were usually to the left side of the face (delivered by a right-handed opponent) and were proudly exhibited. Courage was still required: noses and ears were still occasionally sliced off. The student *Mensur* survived the onset of the First World War and continued into the Weimar Republic. However, the relationship of the student societies with the emerging National Socialist regime was strained. On the one hand, the Nazis were inclined to celebrate activities that showed the courage and the superiority of the national character; on the other they were suspicious of the aristocratic ethos of the societies and the cult of individualism upon which the *Mensur* was predicated. The *Mensur* was banned in 1937. After the war, and on much the same grounds, the East German authorities suppressed the activity, but in West Germany it was revived and formally legalised as a sport. Today, there remain dozens of student societies located in old university towns such as Heidelberg in which the *Mensur* is still occasionally practised. Scars are acquired, though fatalities no longer occur. The societies remain somewhat controversial because of their alleged association with right-wing politics.

The student *Mensur* is the only vestigial remains of a phenomenon once observable throughout European society. The demise of the duel should perhaps not be lamented though, for true duelling was a brutal business and one which led many a young man to an untimely end, often for the most trivial of reasons. If the duel is gone, it has not yet relinquished its hold upon our imaginations, being endlessly replicated in our art and our literature.

FURTHER READING

Baldick, Robert. *The Duel: A History of Duelling*. Chapman and Hall, 1965.

Banks, Stephen. *Killing with Courtesy: The Duel and the English Gentleman*, Boydell, 2010.

Banks, Stephen. 'Killing With Courtesy: the English Duelist, 1785–1845', *Journal of British Studies*, 47 (2008), pp. 528–58.

Banks, Stephen. 'Dangerous friends: the second and the later English duel', *Journal for Eighteenth Century Studies*, 32.1 (2009), pp. 87–106.

Barry, M. *An Affair of Honour: Irish Duels and Duellists*, Eigse Books, 1981.

Billacois, François. *The Duel: Its Rise and Fall in Early Modern France*, ed. and trans. Tristan Selous, Yale University Press, 1990.

David, S. *The Homicidal Earl: The Life of Lord Cardigan*. Abacus, 1997.

Elsmley, Clive. *British Society and the French Wars 1793–1815*. Macmillan, 1979.

Frevert, Ute. *Men of Honour: A Social and Cultural History of the Duel*. Polity Press, 1995.

Hughes, Steven. 'Men of Steel: Dueling, Honor and Politics in Liberal Italy', in *Men and Violence: Gender, Honor and Rituals in Modern Europe and America*, edited by P. Spierenburg, 1989.

Kelly, James. *That Damn'd Thing Called Honour: Duelling in Ireland 1570–1860*. Cork University Press, 1995.

Kiernan, Victor G. *The Duel in European History: Honour and the Reign of Aristocracy*. Oxford University Press, 1988.

Landale, J. *Duel: A True Story of Death and Honour*. Canongate, 2005.

Loose, Jacqueline. *Duels and Duelling: Affairs of Honour around the Wandsworth Area*. Wandsworth Borough Council, 1983.

Low, Jennifer. *Manhood and the Duel: Masculinity in Early Modern Drama*. Palgrave Macmillan, 2003.

McAleer, Kevin. *Dueling: The Cult of Honor in Fin-de-Siècle Germany*. Princeton University Press, 1994.

Manning, Roger B. *Swordsmen: The Martial Ethos in the Three Kingdoms*. Oxford University Press, 2003.

Peltonen, Markku. *The Duel in Early Modern England: Civility, Politeness and Honour*. Cambridge University Press, 2003.

Reid, J. C. *Bucks and Bruisers: Pierce Egan and Regency England*. Routledge, 1971.

Shoemaker, Robert B. *The London Mob: Violence and Disorder in Eighteenth-Century England*. Hambledon, 2004.

Tolstoy, Nikolai. *The Half-Mad Lord: Thomas Pitt, 2nd Baron Camelford*. Holt, Rinehart and Winston, 1978.

Wrigley, E. A. *People, Cities and Wealth: The Transformation of Traditional Society*. Blackwell, 1987.

INDEX

Page numbers in italics
refer to illustrations

Achilles 4, *4*
Adolphus, Gustavus 21
Alis, Harry 49, *50*
Allen, Rev. 42
Almack's 33, *33, 34*
America 31
Armour 7, 12, *12*
Athena 4, *4*
Bacon, Sir Francis
18–19, *18*
Bagger, Austin 17
Bannockburn 7, *8*
Barthelemy, Emmanuel
45
Baynard, Godefroy 6
Beowulf 5
Best, Captain 39
Bond, Mr 41
Bonetti, Rocco 16–17
Book of the Courtier 14,
15–16
Bosquett, Abraham 25
Boucmel, Jean 9
Bouteville, Comte de
47,
Broadswords *19*
Bruce, Robert 7, 8
Buckingham, Duke of
23
Byron, 5th Lord 24
Camelford, Thomas
Pitt, Baron 38–9,
38, 39
Cardigan, James
Brudenell, Lord 44,
45
Casanova, Giovanni,
Giacomo *cover*
Cassation, Court of 47
Charles I 21
Charles II 23
Charles V (Holy Roman
Emperor) *48*
Chivalry 7, 9, 13, 15,
33
Clemenceau, Georges

46, 49
Clifford, Nicholas 8, *9*
Clonmel Code 26
Cockburn, John 27
Coffee house 25, *26*
Cornet, Lieutenant
Frederic 45
Cromwell, Oliver 22
D'Eu, Count 6
De Bohun, Henry 7,8
De Essex, Baron Henry
6
De Lindsay, Sir David 9
De Montford, Robert 6
De Montgomery,
Gabriel, Comte 12
Déroulède, Monsieur
46, 49
Dion, Marquis of *51*
Doctors 31
Dudley, Henry Bate 42,
42
Dulany, Lieutenant 42
Eldon, Lord 31, *32*
Elizabeth I 13, 17
Execution 18, 21, 47
Fawcett, Colonel 44
Fencing 16–17, 24, *25,*
28, 47, *53, 54*
Fighting (fisticuffs) *34*
Firearms, 12, *13*
First World War 52
Fox, Charles James 33
France 6, 9, 17, 23, 38,
44, 47, 51
Francis, Sir Philip *31*
Franco-Prussian War 52
Gambling 33–4, *34*
Gelli, Iacopo 49
Gentlemen 15, *16,*
17, 19, *19,* 21–2, *22,*
24, 27–8, 31–3, *32,*
41–4.
George III 38
Germany 11, 52, 54
Gillray, James 39
Gladiators 5, *5*
Gower, Mr 24
Hamilton, Duke of
23–4, *24*
Hastings, Warren *31*

Hector 4, *4*
Henri II (of France) *9,*
12, 47
Henri IV (of France) 17
Henry II 6
Henry, Colonel 49
Homer 4
Honour 8, 15–16,
18–19, 21, 25–6,
28–9, 31, 33, 35, 38,
41–2, 45, 47–8,
50–2
Hunting 41
Iliad 4
Italy 15–18, 47–9, 50
James I 17–19, 21, 47
James II 23
Jarnac, Guy Chabot,
Baron 47, *49*
Knight 6, *6,* 7, 9, *10,*
11, 12, *12*
La Châtaigneraie,
François de Vivonne
47, *49*
Lateran Council 13
Lawyers 17, 29, 31, 48
Le Chatelier, Monsieur
49–50, *50*
Louis XIII (of France)
47
Maccartney, George
23–4
Manchester 42
Mensur 53, *53,* 54
Mohun, Charles, Baron
23–4, *23,* 24
Moll's Coffee House 26
Norbury, Lord 29
Northampton, Earl of
18
Officers 16, 23, 29, 32,
39, 41–2, 44–5, 52
Oneby, Major 24
Parker, Sir James 12
Picquart, Monsieur 49
Pistol 26–9, *29, 30, 36,*
42, 47–9, 51
Prussia 50, 52
Prussian officer *52*
Richard, Gerault *51*
Robson, Simon 16

Rome 4, 5
Royalists *22*
Salisbury, Bishop of 7
Sanquhar, Lord 17–18
Saviolo, Vincento 17
Schläger 54
Second World War 53
Selden, John 16
Sheridan, Richard
Brinsley 27, 38
Shrewsbury, Earl of 23
Silver, George 17
Stanhope, Hester 39
Star Chamber 17
Stoney, Captain 27
Students 17, 31, *52,*
53, *53,* 54, *54*
Swords 8, 15–16,
19, 20, 21, 22,
24, 27, 47
Theatre 22, 33, 35, *35*
Thirty Years' War 50
Thurlow, Sir Edward
23
Tournament 7, 8, 9, *9,*
11,
Townshend, George 41
Trial 6–7
Trial by battle 6, 7, 9,
13
Tuckett, Harvey 44
Twain, Mark 50
Vaughan, Sir Hugh 12
Victoria, Queen 21, 42
Warden, Mr 41
Watch (night watch) *32*
Welles, Lord 9
Wellesley-Pole Mr 38
Wellington, Duke of
43–4, *43*
Westminster Hall 18,
25, 44
Wilkes, John 35, *38*
William III 23
William Rufus 6
Winchilsea, Lord 43–4
Women 28, 33, 35,
38–9, 52–3
Zola, Émile 49